Graceful Passages

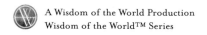 A Wisdom of the World Production
Wisdom of the World™ Series

 New World Library
14 Pamaron Way
Novato, California 94949

©℗ 2003 Wisdom of the World, Inc.
All music published by Companion Arts Music, ASCAP

Speakers' and writers' words used by permission
Text compiled and written by Michael Stillwater
Design © 2003 Michele Wetherbee
Photography © 2000 Daniel Proctor
Epilogue © 1998 KDS, used by permission
Special thanks to the Nathan Cummings Foundation

Library of Congress Cataloging-in-Publication Data
available on request.

First printing, October 2003
Printed in China
Distributed to the trade by Publishers Group West
ISBN-10: 1-57731-561-8
ISBN-13: 978-1-57731-561-2

10 9 8 7 6 5 4 3

Graceful Passages

A COMPANION FOR LIVING AND DYING

Michael Stillwater and Gary Malkin
Music Composed, Conducted, and Produced by Gary Malkin

With messages from leading speakers of the world

New World Library
Novato, California

REFLECTION

on the Tranquility
of Falling Cherry Blossoms

FOR A MOMENT THEY HOVER LIKE BEJEWELLED CLOUDS

AND DANCE ABOVE THE CRYSTAL STREAMS;

THEN, AS THEY SAIL AWAY ON THE LAUGHING WATERS,

THEY SEEM TO SAY:

"FAREWELL, O SPRING! WE ARE ON TO ETERNITY."

— OKAKURA KAKUZO

Dedicated to all who journey into the light of their deepest
longing, and all who help them on their way.

In loving memory of Irving Malkin and William Alexander Korns

C O N T E N T S

PAGE

WHITHER SHALL I GO FROM THY SPIRIT?

Sam Keen

When it comes to dying, I'm an amateur. I haven't done it—I think when I come to do it, I will still be an amateur, somewhere between frightened and terrified. I know that everything I have been in my life will come up before me. I will need comfort and reassurance, and certain things I know will help me to die.

One will be thinking about my family and my friends, and the love that I have given and received. It will help me also to think about my works and my vocation, because that's been a source of great joy to me. I also will think about all the beauty I have tasted, and the beauty of the world, knowing that no matter how old I am, I will lament leaving the wondrous beauty of this world. It will be a struggle to trust that what lies ahead is anything as marvelous as what is behind, the gift of this life.

I've been a person who's been on a religious quest my entire life. This is not new with me; I was almost born doing it. I have studied many of the great religions, and for me, there is one great scripture in all of the literature of the world, one that I want read to me as I'm dying.

This is my scripture, and it's Psalm 139.

Wither shall I go from Thy Spirit,
*   or wither shall I flee from Thy Presence?*
If I shall ascend up into heaven, Thou art there.
If I make my bed in hell, behold, Thou art there.
If I take the wings of the morning
*   and dwell in the uttermost parts of the sea,*
Even there shall Thy hand lead me and Thy right hand
*   shall hold me.*

—EXCERPT FROM PSALM 139, KING JAMES VERSION

The reason this is my scripture is because it's the deepest experience I have that whoever it is that I am, however it is that I came to be—through the DNA, the process of coming through my mother's womb and into this world—there has always been a sense of guidance and purpose both behind and before me.

Even when I have been in despair, there is something deeper down, some kind of trust beneath all the doubt, beneath the anxiety, beneath the fear; I am encompassed by that great reality that can never be named, which therefore we call God.

Those of us working in the field of end-of-life care are often frustrated by the limited expertise available to assist people with the emotional, psychological, and spiritual challenges that an expected dying represents. Even in clinical settings in which sophisticated symptom management is available, these deeply personal aspects of dying are often neglected—unless the person's distress reaches disruptive or psychiatric proportions.

Graceful Passages is a unique resource for people who are facing the prospect of dying. This book and recording makes the wisdom of experienced clinicians, counselors, and spiritual advisors available to anyone who is confronting life's end, either themselves or within their circle of family and friends. In contrast to our medical response to people who are dying, the listener's feelings need not be pathologic before *Graceful Passages* would have value, nor must this soothing resource be prescribed.

Instead, *Graceful Passages* offers anticipatory guidance that is appropriate for anyone interested in exploring their personal mortality. Having listened to the CD, I can attest to the power of the words and music to comfort, build con-fidence, and connect listeners with their own inner wisdom.

Modern individuals are cut adrift to wander without guidance,
without models and without assistance through the varied life stages.
Thus change . . . is often experienced in frightening and isolating
ways, for there are no rites of passage and little help from one's
peers, who are equally adrift.
—JAMES HOLLIS, PH.D., *The Middle Passage*

ACCEPTING OUR MORTALITY, APPRECIATING THE MYSTERY

The wonder of life is often overlooked. The preciousness of being alive, of appreciating ourselves, each other, and our world, is sometimes the last thing we remember in our rush to handle the details of daily life. Yet remembering the fragility of our days awakens us to the truth that in every moment we are dying to something, and ultimately we, and everyone we know, will leave this world entirely.

Acknowledging the inevitable can be healing. Despite tremendous advances in medical science, we are neither capable of preventing our final transition from this world nor in full control of the timing. As reluctant as we may be to approach the subject, accepting our mortality is an important step toward embracing life on its own terms, and recognizing the moment-by-moment gift that is life.

The poet David Whyte speaks of our culture's obsession with what he calls "the bright side of the moon," those attributes of youth, good looks, and success that buffer us from facing the moonless night of loss and mortality. For those of us who have lost our jobs, experienced the breakup of a loving relationship, been diagnosed with a serious illness, or have had to face the death of a loved one, the dark side of the moon is not far away. The comfort of things transpiring according to our wishes is shaken, the sense of order that kept chaos at bay is breached. Life continually carves into, and ultimately washes away, our carefully developed and guarded self.

When we are faced with major change, whether in relationships, finances, career, or health, certain responses may arise. Elisabeth Kübler-Ross categorized them as the "five stages of grief":

1 *Denial.* We may dig in our heels and refuse to accept that something has changed.
2 *Anger.* We might rail at people or institutions, at the audacity of life, or God, for handing us something different from what we want.
3 *Bargaining.* We can try to make a deal with life, the universe, or a Higher Power, hoping to get what we want.
4 *Depression.* We could feel that everything is futile when we sense our underlying helplessness.
5 *Acceptance.* Often only after we have exhausted each of the former responses are we ready to accept that change has occurred.

Waning into darkness each month, the lunar cycle reminds us of a natural progression constantly repeating itself. We may not want summer to end, yet winter comes, revealing a different landscape altogether. Even the most glorious day turns to night, requiring us to adapt to a different kind of light.

The contemplation of change, or the impermanence of the physical world, has been a practice for those on a quest for truth in every age and tradition. The Buddhists say that we start preparing for our dying from the moment we are born. Christian monastics reflect on mortality as a pathway to leading a sacred life. To inquire into the impermanent nature of things is a sign of spiritual intelligence and a gateway to wisdom.

It is perfectly normal as human beings to be attached to, and identified with, that which is familiar. The instinct for survival compels us to resist as long as possible any intrusion into the way we think things "should be." We are endlessly resourceful in attempting possible solutions to difficult problems. But resistance itself cannot make things different from the way they are.

To ask for what we want is human. To be willing to receive what comes is grace. While we cannot resist the natural course of change, we can choose to pass through it gracefully. *Graceful Passages* was conceived as a tool to support those who are seeking the serenity that comes with acceptance.

With every loss, we are faced with the fragility of our situation. We die a little every day. In countless minor and sometimes major ways, we lose control over and over again. How we respond to this continuous process is our preparation for how we will face our own eventual death, as well as how we meet others during their times of transition. To enfold the process of dying in the embrace of living is a challenge that faces us, both individually and as a society.

In this book—and on the accompanying CD—Alan Jones, Dean of Grace Cathedral in San Francisco, says,

"We practice dying every day so we can be fully alive." By facing our fears of dying, and making peace with our own life journey, we can have a more spacious, free, and joyful existence. Embracing our losses, our little deaths, rather than resisting them, strengthens our courage to more easily accept when surrender is the only option.

EMBRACING THE TRANSITIONS OF OUR LIVES

The passages of our life call for recognition; they are an invitation to reflection, an opportunity for conscious change often overlooked in our modern world. Birth, entering into intimacy, illness, loss of loved ones, dying— all lead us to our most vulnerable self. Regardless of background, faith, ethnicity, or belief system, we are all subject to the challenges that accompany change.

Wherever we are in our life cycle, when in the midst of transition we may feel like travelers without a map or compass. While traditional cultures provide ceremonial initiations and guidance, many of us today feel bereft of such grounding elements. Without spiritual direction or mentoring, we are left to our own devices to find meaning in the chaos that transition often stirs up.

When we first created *Graceful Passages*, Gary Malkin and I intended to offer comfort and inspiration from various viewpoints to ease the anxieties that so often surround the ultimate transition—dying. We wanted the music and messages to be a bridge of wisdom to those preparing for or helping others in the midst of dying, and we are grateful that this prayer has been fulfilled in so many ways.

Beyond this original intention, however, we have heard from people who have found other uses. Whether for meditation, therapy, ceremonial gatherings, family bonding, as audio-enhancement for lectures or classes, workshops and retreats, or a gift for employees or loved ones, *Graceful Passages* is being used as an accompaniment to all phases of life, and often as a catalyst for more meaningful experiences of transition.

A young man wrote, "I literally listen to it every

night. . . . Being that I'm still under thirty, I use *Graceful Passages* as a meditation to help me prepare for what is to come beyond this journey." An eleven-year-old wrote of how it helped shift her attitude, saying that listening to *Graceful Passages* during a hard time in life "soothed my soul of all hatred."

Of all the transitions we pass through, the death of our physical body is often the most frightening, perhaps because what lies beyond is so mysterious and unknown. As the young man quoted above so wisely understood, we can prepare for our death as we traverse the innumerable "little deaths," the losses and transitions we face throughout our lives.

The spoken messages can be understood both literally and metaphorically. When you hear the word *dying,* consider any change you are facing—the ending of a phase of your life, the letting go of a relationship or career. When you hear Lew Epstein saying farewell to his loved ones, you may use the opportunity to ask who in your life might benefit from your love and appreciation, right now. What feelings emerge as you imagine saying good-bye to them? Recognizing the little deaths throughout our lives is a spiritual practice that cultivates gratitude for all our life experiences and genuinely prepares us for our final letting go.

As we feel deeply met in our transitions, we in turn develop our capacity to meet others during their challenging times. May *Graceful Passages* help us all to grow in presence, empathy, and compassion, qualities that serve us in whatever transitions we are passing through in our lives.

THE PURPOSE OF GRACEFUL PASSAGES

How do we bring beauty and dignity to our endings? How do we best honor sacred traditions, and yet leave room for the mystery beyond any pathway? How might we meet each other during our times of dying—whether they are emotional, physical, or spiritual—in the deepest way possible, allowing whatever is happening to take place without intruding or assuming? *Graceful Passages* is the result of three years spent exploring these questions, and we offer it to gently engage you and your loved ones in your own inquiry, and to provide support as you explore the thoughts and feelings that might arise when asking such questions.

Many of those who offered their wisdom for *Graceful Passages* are foremost experts in the field of loss and transition. Others are teachers who embody a lifetime of compassionate service. All of them know loss firsthand. They speak candidly, inspired by the moment. The themes they share are relevant at any stage of letting go— giving and receiving love, the benefits of forgiveness and appreciation, the power of conscious closure. They offer various viewpoints on the continuity of spirit, addressing the mystery of our ongoing journey.

Coming from different traditions, these guides share

an extraordinary quality of presence that infuses their words with a tender, universal eloquence. The messages they deliver are enhanced by a musical accompaniment composed to support profound transitions by gently addressing the listener beyond habitual defenses.

The words and music of *Graceful Passages* provide support for anyone, whatever transition he or she may be facing, to contemplate what is most deeply valuable. May this offering encourage reconciliation, resolution, and peaceful transitions throughout your life.

AIR TO BREATHE, LIGHT TO SEE.

A SOUL NEEDS NOURISHMENT ALL ITS OWN.

WHOEVER YOU ARE, WHEREVER YOU'RE FROM,

WHATEVER TRADITION GUIDES YOUR WAY,

THERE COMES A TIME WHEN WE ALL NEED

TO BE TOUCHED THROUGH THE HEART.

LETTING YOURSELF BE LOVED

Lew Epstein | *Lessons from the heart—cultivating*
inner peace through receiving love.

No one has ever prepared us for this experience.
We think it's the end—no.
It's another beginning.
It's knowing that you're loved, knowing that you're loved.
It's not easy, letting yourself be loved—
Because we've learned to judge ourselves—
    we're always judging ourselves.

But I learned to listen that I was loved. I was loved!
And then I would forget that I was loved.
Those were the most painful times for me—
    forgetting that I was loved.

So you've let yourself be loved while you've been here.
And you judged yourself.
And you've forgotten that you were loved.
And you became alone . . . but you will always be here.

You are blessed. You are forgiven. You are an angel.

You have to listen that you're loved and you have to
    forgive all the time.
Listen that you're loved and forgive, all the time.
You are love.

Farewell my son.
Farewell my daughter.
Farewell my father.
Farewell my mother.
Farewell my sister.
Farewell my brother.

Thank you for letting me love you.
Thank you for letting yourself be loved.
God bless you.

> *Lew Epstein, whose loving words live on in the hearts of all who
> hear them, made his graceful passage on March 28, 2003.*

RETURNING HOME

Tu Weiming | *A Confucian wisdomkeeper invites us to consider our unique place in the cosmos.*

Your vital energy is returning to the Source,
Like the flowing stream returning to ocean.

Heaven is our Father, Earth is our Mother,
All people are our brothers and sisters,
and all things are our companions.

In this gentle, peaceful journey,
You are forming one body with heaven
    and earth.
Entrust yourself in the transforming and
    nourishing care of the Cosmos.
Listen to the voice of love in silence.
You have heard the Way;
Return Home in Peace.

An Episcopal priest speaks of his daily practice in the art of "contemplative dying." | The Very Rev. Alan Jones

Thou has seen and known my heart, seeing into every part
Nothing hidden here from Thee, ever Thou embraceth me
Even deep in darkest night, Thou would guide me with Thy Light

In my tradition we try to practice dying every day so that we may be fully alive. What I understand of my prayer life is to place myself on the threshold of death, to participate in my dying, so that I may live each day and each moment as a gift. What I cultivate is a grateful heart; each moment then becomes a new thing. My gratitude comes from the sheer gift of life itself.

Who you are cannot be contained in what is happening to you just now. You are part of a love story. You are desired and longed for. There are thousands of witnesses before you who would claim that you are held in the arms of love. And I'd like to leave you with the prayer that one of the Franciscans left with me—

O my God, you are here. O my God, I am here. O my God, we are here.
And always, always you love us. Always, always you love us.

May the angels of God watch over you; may Mary and all the Saints pray for you, and all those whose lives you touch, Now and forevermore, Amen.

WALK ON

Jyoti | *We witness a lifetime through the eyes of one deeply connected to the Earth.*

Good morning, Grandfather.
I entered this life a ways back
and put skin on to walk two-legged on this Creation—
and what a glorious time it was.

It taught me about breath
and about sensing and feeling and caring through my heart.
And I walked on around that Red Road,
looking and trying to understand more
about the mystery and the secrets She holds.

And You spoke to me through the wind,
and You sang to me through the birds.
And You brought challenges forth so that
I might listen to the message You bring me more sincerely.
And I kept walking down this road.

And I came 'round the bend
at the middle of that curve in the road
and I began to find a secret in the Spirit of my Self...

And still I walked on, sometimes blind and deaf,
and sometimes with pain.
But I fought with my fears and I embraced my unknowingness—
and still I walked on.
And my children and my family stood with me
and we came to know each other in those later years more than we
had before—for some of our falseness had fallen away—
and still I walked on.

And I kept walking on this road towards You,
towards that other world that grew closer to me with each step.
And as the door of the Great Spirit world came closer
my fear loomed up inside sometimes. . . .

But something called me forth—
the Morning Star rose with each day—
and my prayer became a centering—and still I walked on,
until I began to hear the Song of the Mother,
and Her arms embraced me so,
that instead of walking She carried me right to the door.
And as the door opened, I heard Her Song,
And Her Song lifted me up, so I could soar.

THE END OF SUFFERING

Thich Nhat Hanh | *We are invited by a Buddhist*
master to relax into peacefulness.

May the sound of this bell penetrate deep into the cosmos
Even in the darkest spots living beings are able to hear it clearly
So that all suffering in them cease, understanding come to
    their heart
And they transcend the path of sorrow and death.

The universal dharma door is already open
The sound of the rising tide is heard clearly
The miracle happens
A beautiful child appears in the heart of the lotus flower
One single drop of this compassionate water is enough
to bring back the refreshing spring to our mountains
    and rivers.

Listening to the bell I feel the afflictions in me begin to dissolve
My mind calm, my body relaxed
A smile is born on my lips
Following the sound of the bell, my breath brings me back
to the safe island of mindfulness
In the garden of my heart, the flowers of peace bloom
    beautifully.

FRANCISCAN BLESSING

A monk from Assisi, Italy, gives us a blessing from the heart of St. Francis. | Fr. Maximillian Mizzi, O.F.M. Conv.

May the Lord bless you and keep you
May He turn His face on you and give you His peace
And His joy, and His love, and His protection
May He be with you now at this hour, and every moment of
    your life
At the moment when you close your eyes
In order to open them to Him, to His Glory
May He be with you, May He bless you,
The Father, the Son and the Holy Spirit. Amen.

    Our Father, Who Art in heaven
    Hallowed be Thy Name
    Thy Kingdom come, Thy Will be done
    On earth as it is in heaven
    Give us this day our daily bread
    And forgive us our trespasses,
    As we forgive those who trespass against us
    And lead us not into temptation, but deliver us from evil
    For Thine is the kingdom, and the power, and the glory, forever, amen

Help us Lord, bless us Lord, thank You Lord. Amen.

IN YOUR BLESSED HANDS

Rabbi Zalman Schachter-Shalomi | *We witness a sacred conversation*
between the Jewish Rabbi and his God.

God, You made me from before I was born.
You took me through my life.
You supported me.
You were there with me when I wasn't there with You.
There were times I was sick and You healed me.
There were times I was in despair and You gave me hope.
There were times when I felt betrayed and I could still turn to You.

It was a wonderful life. I loved and I was loved.
I sang, I heard music, I saw flowers, I saw sunrises and sunsets.
Even in places when I was alone,
You, in my heart, helped me turn loneliness into precious solitude.
And I look back over the panorama of my life,
What a wonderful privilege this was!

I still have some concerns for people in the family,
    for the world, for the planet.
I put them in Your Blessed Hands.
I trust that whatever in the web of life that needed me to be
    there is now completed.
I thank You for taking the burden from me,
And I thank You for keeping me in the Light.
As I let go, and let go . . . and let go.

UNCONDITIONAL LOVE

A pioneer of transitions shares her deepest understanding of what is most important in life. | Elisabeth Kübler-Ross, M.D.

Look forward to your transition.
It's the first time you will experience unconditional love.
There will be all peace and love, and all the nightmares and the
　　turmoil you went through in your life will be like nothing.
When you make your transition you are asked two things basically:
How much love you have been able to give and receive,
　　and how much service you have rendered.
And you will know every consequence of every deed, every thought,
　　and every word you have ever uttered.
And that is, symbolically speaking, going through hell
　　when you see how many chances you have missed.
But you also see how a nice act of kindness
　　has touched hundreds of lives that you're totally unaware of.
So concentrate on love while you're still around,
　　and teach your children early unconditional love.
So remember, concentrate on love, and look forward to the
　　transition.
It's the most beautiful experience you can ever imagine.
Vayas con Dios!

Arun and Sunanda Gandhi | *She speaks from wisdom gained by her near-death experience;*
he recalls a vision shared by his grandfather, Mahatma Gandhi.

SUNANDA:

I know what it means to go. I know all of us have to go away
  one day.
I have had an experience of near death. I have come back.
But I am going one day.
We are not alone—we are with Him or Her, the Spirit.

ARUN:

My grandfather, Mohandas Karamchand Gandhi, used to
  say that physical death is the birth of spiritual life.
He felt that, since light is enlightenment
  and also a life-giving source,
that when we die, we all merge into the great Sun or the Moon,
because they are the celestial lights, that give us life—
  and they take us back again.

SUNANDA:

We are not alone—we are with Him or Her, the Spirit.

ARUN:

Give us life—and take us back again.

An American spiritual teacher speaks | Ram Dass
of experiences beyond this world.

Be here now.
Don't anticipate, don't yearn for things of the past.
Let the past go with forgiveness
    and let the future go with no anticipation.

Each of us contains a being that doesn't die and a being that
    does die.[1]
Everything must change except the soul.[2]
Your preparation for dying is done by identifying with
    your soul, not your ego. Identify with your soul now.

There are realms other than the one we are meeting on.
Planes where we see the souls that we have known in the past
    as just souls.
We won't meet them in their clothing of mother or father,
    or uncle or aunt.

Then . . . sensual planes, planes with color, music. . . .

Planes which have no form. . . .
This plane is where all of it starts.
This plane is the womb, the beginning of things.
This plane is ecstatic. It's the ultimate creativity.

Dying is the most important moment that exists in any
    incarnation.
It's important that you not be so overwhelmed by the
    processes of dying.

I wish you a process for dying that doesn't overwhelm you.
I wish you a moment of dying that you can be conscious of.
I wish you a future incarnation in a plane of incredible light.

[1] The one who dies may also be described as an identification of the being,
not the being itself.

[2] Soul, as described here, refers to the immortal, unchanging dimension of
self, the true self, or atman, as distinct from the concept of a soul which
grows through a lifetime (or lifetimes) of experience.

Michael Stillwater

*A guided journey of relaxation, transitioning into a heavenly
soundscape, then emerging into a song of homecoming*

Let yourself relax into this moment.
Let yourself be held without any need to hold yourself up.
Let yourself meet the unknown.
It's OK. It's a place we don't have to know with our mind.

What if there were angels all around you
    and you just couldn't see them?
What if there was a love so vast that you could never be apart
    from it?
What if it was impossible for you to go anywhere
Where this love could not find you?

You are entering the Beauty not far from your heart.
It's a place that embraces you as you are.
I trust that you will be met by a welcoming presence
    that knows you, and that meets you with a deeper love
    than you have ever imagined in this world.

May you know, without any doubt, the precious gift that
    you are.
And may you be welcomed by a presence so loving that all
    fear subsides.

Far beyond where winds have blown, waking into realms unknown
Footsteps free of space and time, silent thunder, holy mind
In the heart a song of peace and mercy calling me back home.

SWING LOW, SWEET CHARIOT

A lullaby-like gospel of heavenly | Linda Tillery
promise from the soul of a great singer

Swing low,
Sweet Chariot
Coming for to carry
me home.

Swing low,
Sweet Chariot
Coming for to carry
me home.

ENDING PRAYER

Kathleen Dowling Singh, Ph.D.

It has long been my prayer that we will offer each other loving and skillful means in the process of dying and at the time of death. I also pray that we will be compassionate with one another during the challenging transitions of our lives. This endeavor, *Graceful Passages*, is such a loving and skillful means, filled with compassion and insight into the rich and sacred transition of dying, whether literal or metaphoric. Every dying person is naturally being drawn within and on to the beyond, naturally hearing the call to remerge with the Ground of Being. This is also true, on some level, for everyone facing the "little deaths" of unexpected outcomes that weave throughout our lives.

What begins to emerge as necessary, during these times, are simple yet essential things: the good, the true, the beautiful. Let these messages and this music, along with our love, accompany all who need comfort and companionship. With these words and music, and with our love, let us create the environment and conditions that nurture movement through the profound spiritual transformations of dying.

PRAYER FOR PRESENCE

Let us be the ear that listens without judgment and with deep compassion to all that the voice of our loved one has to say in the phase of Chaos.

Let us be the still and quiet point of acceptance where the personal life is reviewed and resolved, honored and released.

Let us be the silent and understanding companion to the voiceless time of Surrender.

The love will endure, never fear. In fact, beyond the personal self, love just gets stronger, purer, freer, deeper.

Go there with your loved one.

Sit and breathe with your loved one, matching your rhythms.

Sit and meditate with your loved one, matching your visions.

Sit and pray with your loved one, matching your deepest longings.

Let us share, far beyond the last breath and even through a breaking heart, in our loved one's Transcendence: the entrance, at the edge of life, into the peaceful and luminous Center.

GRACE IN PRACTICE

Michael Stillwater and Gary Malkin

Graceful Passages has touched a wide audience. The stories we have heard from readers and listeners are rich with meaning and poignant in their sincerity. They portray a wide variety of uses and potential benefits, delivering a testament of love, forgiveness, reconciliation, and living more fully in the present.

Whether from a Montana family gathered around a dying parent, a New York executive moved to tears after hearing the music played to him by an associate, or a California chaplain witnessing breakthroughs between family members, the letters and calls we receive all acknowledge the comforting and healing power of this work. Hearing these stories is convincing evidence of the relevance that *Graceful Passages* holds, not only for those at the end of life but for anyone living through these times of increased uncertainty.

When one opens to what we call the "healing power of acceptance," stress levels often decrease and immune systems are strengthened by a greater peace of mind. Family members, who so often feel concerned, helpless, and upset about the condition of their loved ones, can benefit from healing words and music that soothe the nerves and allow them to be more of a comforting presence for the person facing the health challenge.

The wisdom of *Graceful Passages* is perceived through the senses, felt through the heart, and recognized by the soul. While its impact can be profound for the individual upon first listening, the effect only increases as it is shared with partners, family, friends, associates, clients, or patients.

We have heard from many families who have used the music and words during the dying process of a loved one. For some, *Graceful Passages* has been woven into the experience for weeks or even months of an extended period of releasing. For others, it has been introduced in the last days or hours before death. We always hear a sense of grace and gratitude for the way that *Graceful Passages* helped reveal the dying experience for the sacred event it is, and helped evoke a moment surrounded, whenever possible, by beauty and peace.

In comforting the recently bereaved, *Graceful Passages* provides a sanctuary that supports listeners in being present with their feelings of grief. Many have written to us or told us about a renewed faith in the continuity of spirit, and a comfort in the belief that, though unseen, their loved ones are still present.

We also hear from those whose grief is not recent, but from years past. This unexpressed grief may be hidden away in the heart, waiting for the safety and invitation of the "right" circumstances for expression. Sometimes, *Graceful Passages* becomes the catalyst for providing such a moment.

Listeners respond because of the beauty of the music and the wisdom of the words, and because of the way it helps them carry on with their lives as it assists them in letting go.

On many occasions, *Graceful Passages* has been given as a gift to honor the passing of a loved one. On some occasions the magnitude of loss is staggering, yet even then it can help in some way to bring a tender note of acknowledgement and recognition to the moment.

My brother founded a company which lost thirty employees who worked on an upper floor of the World Trade Center. Last weekend we honored the family members at a memorial service. I was asked to speak, and talked about their courage and dedication, and of the terrible loss each person had suffered, how none of our lives would ever be the same. Later we introduced the concept behind Graceful Passages, *and that this would be a gift to each of the families that had touched our lives over the fifteen years of the company's existence. After the service we had dinner for all of the families. As I walked around and talked with each family, I gave each of them their copy . . . thank you for creating this gift to the world.*

In Healthcare

Graceful Passages has been recognized as an innovative healthcare resource by Bill Moyers in his landmark PBS series on dying in America, *On Our Own Terms*. It is now used in daily service in hundreds of hospices, palliative care clinics, and cancer centers providing comfort to patients and families. Time and again, it has helped people deal with the critical issues of closure, forgiveness, and spirituality. Perhaps the most meaningful benefit has been helping both patient and care-giver become less afraid of the unknown.

We continue to receive heartfelt stories from a wide array of both mainstream and complementary healthcare organizations in America and abroad describing the effectiveness of *Graceful Passages* for reducing anxieties and enhancing the quality of caregiving. In a field notorious for stress and burnout, this resource is providing a much-needed oasis for practitioners to refill their well of meaning and purpose.

A growing trend in healthcare is the acceptance of a nondenominational spirituality, which has been proven to beneficially influence the experience of both care provider and patient. *Graceful Passages* reflects this new awareness in a way that honors many traditions. Clergy and spiritual care providers have found that *Graceful Passages* enhances their ministries and supports them in their counseling of those dealing with fear and loss.

CREATING SACRED SPACE

In contrast to blaring televisions or discordant noises connected with the steady stream of activities in most health-care institutions, a serene audio environment contributes to everyone's peace of mind. Music that conveys beauty and peace promotes healing wherever it is played.

Graceful Passages helps to establish "sacred space." Sacred space can occur anywhere at any time, converting a bedroom or hospital room into a place where appreciation is invited, reconciliation is evoked, and heartfelt prayers are natural. Anyone, including the patient, family members, physicians, nurses, or others are capable at any time of transforming an environment into one conducive for reflective thoughts and meaningful conversations.

Physicians and nurses caring for patients have discovered that *Graceful Passages* helps soften the atmosphere and eases tensions for patients and staff as well, whether using the enclosed messages CD or the companion instrumental CD, *Unspeakable Grace.* Leslie G. Landrum, M.D., at the Circle of Life Hospice expressed it beautifully in her letter to us:

> *The music is beautiful and centering. It is effective for our staff as well as for patients and families. We have used it as background for memorial services that include families and for services that are held to support the hospice staff itself. The meditations have been powerful tools to help find meaning in the transition from life through death. The variety of traditions facilitates our finding one that will be most helpful in specific cases. I cannot emphasize enough how supportive the meditations are for those of us who serve our patients, to help us recharge and refocus on our goals of service, which can sometimes get lost in the chaos that surrounds end-of-life care.* Graceful Passages *is a heart-filling tool for helping our patients and families in life and in death.*

We are profoundly grateful to hear about all the ways in which *Graceful Passages* is having a beneficial influence on the lives of people throughout the world.

Music frees souls, captures and surrenders hearts . . . and hurls the spirit into the infinite.
—JOHN M. ORTIZ, PH.D., author of *The Tao of Music*

Music has a remarkable power. It can create a quality in the air that can unnerve the hardest of hearts. It can catalyze fear, passion, commitment, and even ecstasy. It has also been known to soothe the deepest of wounds and help provide a sanctuary of perspective in times of challenge.

Music has the uncanny ability to create an emotionally rich environment that can profoundly change the way we see and feel things. It reflects where we are at any moment in our lives, while helping us navigate the twists and turns of life.

Although many of us listen to music, rarely do we listen to the kind of music that invites us into the inner sanctum of our hearts and souls. For centuries, most western music known to touch the realms of the Spirit was created in the context of the rituals of religious traditions.

Following in this long-established tradition of sacred music, we set out to create an intimate "audio sanctuary" in which the listener might truly hear, feel, and understand the essence of the speaker's message, while having the freedom to have one's own personal experience simultaneously.

While conceiving the music, we drew upon the art and craft of film scoring. As if the speakers themselves were "movies" to be scored, we listened intently to who they were, what tradition or culture they represented, what their messages were, and how they were delivered. Tu Weiming's embodiment of a true equanimity called out for a warm, confident melody infused with a flavor of the Far East. The Reverend Alan Jones, in his humble declaration of life as a fragile, precious gift, evoked the quality of a liturgical hymn with a familiar, Celtic theme. Ram Dass's exploration into the mysteries of the afterlife resulted in a musical treatment that reflects wonder, awe, and a feeling of unlimited possibilities. As the music was born, we noticed an alchemy that would arise when the intimately spoken word was combined with an appropriately resonant musical score.

While the instrumental music for *Graceful Passages* was originally intended to enhance the spoken word, we discovered a delightful surprise. Upon playing the instrumental music by itself without the speakers' voices (see page 77), we discovered that the music evokes the very qualities of presence, compassion, and authenticity that the speakers expressed. We found that the music encourages people to speak more intimately and deliberately. Exchanges between loved ones become more overtly compassionate. Empathy and connection between people is noticeably enhanced, and conversations start to reflect a greater appreciation for the fragility and preciousness of life.

Of all the many comments and notes of appreciation we have received about *Graceful Passages* (and its companion instrumental CD, *Unspeakable Grace: The Music of* Graceful Passages), one is especially precious to me. A mother wrote to say that she and her seven-year-old daughter had been intently listening one afternoon to the music of *Graceful Passages*. After about twenty minutes, the child began to cry uncontrollably. When she finally calmed down enough to tell her mother what she was feeling, the little girl said, "This must be the music God listens to."

As the composer for *Graceful Passages*, it has been an honor to create music for those engaged in the exploration of life's mysteries. My prayer is that you surround yourself with the music, wherever you might find it, that reminds you of the most beautiful peace possible, the deepest comfort conceivable . . . the music that "God listens to."

Gary Malkin
June 2003

Michael Stillwater

Since my early years I have been drawn to practices for cultivating a peaceful mind and compassionate heart. Quite naturally, my spiritual inclination dovetailed with my interest in music. Soon I knew without a doubt that my music was for healing, and this set me on a journey that led to the creation of *Graceful Passages*. Along the way, I have developed a number of ways to help others calm the restlessness within and find the peace of deep connection. My primary method has included meditation, singing and chanting.

In 1993 I sang to my father during his final transition. The impact of this, for myself and for our relationship, was profound. I experienced firsthand the power of music to guide someone "between worlds." I knew this spiritual midwifery through singing would be a gift to share with others.

I invited Gary Malkin, my longtime friend and musical colleague, to help me produce a recording of my songs "at the threshold." Eventually that CD, *JourneySongs*, was released, and what developed with Gary was an extraordinary collaboration that led to *Graceful Passages*. Gary's beautiful and evocative music perfectly suited the nature of the project. I stepped into the role of producer, interviewing the speakers, editing the messages, and guiding the melding of the words with music.

I have been greatly moved by the wise beings encountered throughout this project. Working with Gary's artistry and dedication has been a true gift, as has been the extraordinary outpouring of goodwill from everyone we met along the way. Originally intended as a resource to support those leaving this earthly life, *Graceful Passages* has turned out to be an inspirational portal for reverently and courageously embracing this world.

Michael Stillwater is a spiritual educator who uses music for healing. He is an award-winning songwriter and recording artist, and his music translates universal spiritual principles into evocative songs and chants. His work is pioneering, offering intuitive songs for patients, caregivers, and medical staff facing end-of-life issues. He is a featured presenter at conferences and provides workshops and retreats supporting the rediscovery of meaning, cultivating presence, and creating sacred space. For more, see www.innerharmony.com.

Gary Malkin

When I was twenty-one years old, I witnessed a horrific accident that resulted in the death of the daughter of my dearest friends. She was a little four-year-old girl I adored. This was my first initiation into the cycles of Life and Death. When I saw her lifeless body at the memorial, I knew with all my being that she was somewhere. Where, I didn't know. But I had a feeling of Knowing that was more profound than I could ever describe in words. She still existed in some realm; of this I was completely certain.

A number of years after that, I had the rare opportunity to be with my father as he faced his final days. He did so with nobility, grace, and gratitude, in the midst of great pain and suffering. After experiencing his death, I could safely say that I would never be the same again. I viscerally understood that we really are here for a very short time, that we are fragile, and that life is precious beyond our imaginings.

So when my dear friend Michael Stillwater, whose own father had recently died, asked if I was interested in collaborating on a project that would support people facing issues of loss and mortality, I felt I had been sufficiently prepared. Throughout my entire life as a musician, my most fervent desire had been to touch people's hearts at the deepest level. For a composer, what could be more gratifying than to use the universal language of music to embrace and support those facing the vast and often frightening unknown? I joined Michael in a creative process in which we discovered this concept of blending intimate spoken messages supported by customized, film-score quality music.

We gathered and edited the voices of the "wisdom keepers," those who have experienced the passages of life. To compose the music to accompany their spoken messages, I listened to them over and over again, soaking in their intent and their inherent quality. Creating music for these voices and listening to them repeatedly provided a healing balm to my soul that has brought forth blessed gratitude, forgiveness, and peace of mind.

Graceful Passages is an offering to all who wish to be deeply met at the doorway of loss. I feel privileged to have worked with Michael and with such magnificent speakers and musicians, creating a work more moving than any one of us could have achieved or envisioned alone. Wherever you are on the continuum of life, my hope for you and your loved ones is that *Graceful Passages* will offer you peace during your times of transition, whatever they may be, and inspire gratitude for the precious gift of life.

Gary Malkin is a composer and producer dedicated to making a difference in the world by participating in projects that catalyze social change and inspire the heart. As principle composer of MUSAIC, his music production company, he has created scores for films with themes on tolerance, the environment, children, and interfaith spirituality. He has received seven Emmys and six ASCAP awards for his work in television and film. He also offers speeches and performances nationwide. He and his daughter live in northern California. For more, see www.musaic.biz.

ABOUT THE SPEAKERS

In order of appearance:

Lew Epstein (1919–2003) was a well-known public speaker for more than fifty years. With his wife Francine, he founded and co-led Men's and Women's Clubs in the United States and Europe on the subject of relationship, and co-founded a nonprofit organization, The Partnership Foundation. He wrote *Trusting You Are Loved: Practices for Partnership.*

The Partnership Foundation
775 E. Blithedale #106, Mill Valley, CA 94941
Tel: (415) 458-1945   tpfmail@aol.com   www.partnership.org

Tu Weiming is Harvard-Yenching Professor of Chinese History and Philosophy and of Confucian Studies, director of the Harvard-Yenching Institute at Harvard University, and a fellow of the American Academy of Arts and Sciences. He interprets Confucian ethics as a spiritual resource for the emerging global community.

Harvard University, 2 Divinity Avenue, Cambridge, MA 02138
Tel: (617) 495-3369   Fax: (617) 495-7798
wtu@fas.harvard.edu   www.fas.harvard.edu/~wtu/index.html

The Very Rev. Alan Jones is Dean of Grace Cathedral in San Francisco. Fr. Jones was the director and founder of the Center for Christian Spirituality at the General Theological Seminary, and is Honorary Canon of Chartres Cathdral in France. His most recent book is *The Soul's Journey: Exploring the Three Passages of Spiritual Life with Dante As a Guide.*

Grace Cathedral, 1100 California Street, San Francisco, CA 94108
www.gracecathedral.org

Jyoti (Jeanine Prevatt, Ph.D.), author of *An Angel Called My Name,* is a devotee of the Mother. Holding sacred her Cherokee lineage, she teaches indigenous spiritual practices that evoke a state of prayer and healing. She is spiritual director and co-founder of Kayumari, a spiritual healing community in northern California, and has served as director of the Spiritual Emergence Network.

Kayumari, Box 1655, Columbia, CA 95310
Tel: (209) 533-8809
office@kayumari.com   www.kayumari.com

Thich Nhat Hanh is a Buddhist monk, poet, peace activist, and the author of *Being Peace, Miracle of Mindfulness,* and many other books and audio projects. Nominated for the Nobel Peace Prize by Martin Luther King Jr., he lives in a monastic community in southern France known as Plum Village, where he teaches, writes, gardens, and works to help refugees worldwide. The singer on this track is Phap Niem, a monk who lives at Plum Village.

Upper Hamlet, Le Pey, 24240, Thenac, France
Tel: (+33) 553-58-4858
UH-office@plumvillage.org   www.plumvillage.org

Fr. Maximilian Mizzi, O.F.M. Conv., is a Franciscan priest from Malta ministering in Assisi, Italy, for the last forty years. He is Delegate General for Ecumenism and Interreligious Dialogue and founder of the International Franciscan Centre for Dialogue, in Assisi. For many years he has been associated with world religious and political leaders to spread the message of peace among people and to dialogue between the world's religions. For this work he has been nominated for the Nobel Peace Prize.

Centro Francescano Internazionale per il Dialogo
Piazzetta Spagnoli, I-06081 Assisi (PG), Italy
Tel: (075) 815 193   Fax: (075) 815 197
maxcefid@krenet.it

Rabbi Zalman Schachter-Shalomi is the founder and president of the trans-denominational Spiritual Eldering Institute, an eminent rabbi and Professor Emeritus of Religion at Temple University, and leader of the Jewish Renewal Movement. He held the World Wisdom Chair at the Naropa Institute from 1996 to 1999 and is currently Professor of Religious Studies there. He is author of *Paradigm Shift, From Age-ing to Sage-ing, Gate to the Heart,* and *Spiritual Intimacy.*

1720 Lehigh Street, Boulder, CO 80303
zalmans@aol.com   www.aleph.org

Elisabeth Kübler-Ross, M.D., is best known as the pioneer and founder of the movement to bring awareness to death and dying in our modern world. A Swiss medical doctor, her best-seller, *On Death and Dying*, was the first of many acclaimed books she wrote on the subject.

www.elisabethkublerross.com

Arun and Sunanda Gandhi are founders of the M.K. Gandhi Institute for Nonviolence. Arun, grandson of Mahatma Gandhi, is also author of five books and co-publisher of the *Suburban Echo* and editor of *World without Violence: Can Gandhi's Dream Become a Reality?*

M.K. Gandhi Institute for Nonviolence
650 East Parkway S., Memphis, TN 38104
Tel: (901) 452-2824
questions@gandhiinstitute.org   www.gandhiinstitute.org

Ram Dass, Ph.D., is an international lecturer, author, and a leading Western exponent of ancient Eastern philosophies. He has founded two organizations, Seva and The Hanuman Foundation, dedicated to promoting social action and to alleviating human suffering. He is author of *Grist for the Mill, Still Here: Embracing Changing, Aging and Dying,* and other books.

Ram Dass Tape Library
524 San Anselmo Avenue, #203, San Anselmo, CA 94960
Tel: (800) 248-1008   www.ramdasstapes.org

Linda Tillery is a vocalist, speaker, producer, arranger, and teacher dedicated to the research, teaching, and performance of the great African American oral tradition, the ancestor of today's American popular song.

Tuizer Music, P.O. Box 11195, Oakland, CA 94611
Tel: (510) 869-3932
tuizer@aol.com   www.culturalheritagechoir.com

ABOUT THE WRITERS

Sam Keen is a well-known speaker, co-producer of an award-winning PBS documentary, and author of many books, including *Fire in the Belly, To Love and Be Loved,* and *Hymns to an Unknown God.*

16331 Norrbom Road, Sonoma, CA 95476

Ira Byock, M.D., is author of *Dying Well*, co-founder and principal investigator of Life's End Institute in Missoula, Montana, and serves as director of the Robert Wood Johnson Foundation National Program Office, Promoting Excellence in End-of-Life Care. He is also past president of the American Academy of Hospice and Palliative Medicine.

www.dyingwell.org

Kathleen Dowling Singh, Ph.D., is a transpersonal psychologist and author of *The Grace in Dying: How We Are Transformed Spiritually As We Die,* as well as numerous articles on the spiritual dimensions of dying. She lectures on death, dying, and spiritual transformation.

SinghKathleen@aol.com

George Washington Institute for Spirituality and Healing
www.gwish.org

Growthhouse
www.growthhouse.org

The Jenna Druck Foundation
www.jennadruck.org

Last Acts: A National Coalition to
Improve Care and Caring at the End of Life
www.lastacts.org

National Family Caregivers Association
www.nfcacares.org

National Hospice and Palliative Care Organization
www.nhpco.org

On Our Own Terms: Moyers on Dying
www.pbs.org/onourownterms

Produced by Michael Stillwater and Gary Malkin
All Music Composed and Arranged by Gary Malkin*

*except for:
Letting Yourself Be Loved and *Walk On*, by Gary Malkin and Dan Alvarez
Water Is Wide, Trad.; lyrics by Michael Stillwater (on *The Gift of Life*)
The End of Suffering, Trad.
The Welcoming, lyrics by Michael Stillwater
He Nay Mah Tov, Trad. (on *In Your Blessed Hands*)
Swing Low, Sweet Chariot, Trad.

Orchestrated and Conducted by Gary Malkin
(except for *The Welcoming*, Greg Sudmeir conducting)

Choir conducted by Marika Kuzma

Co-produced, Engineered, and Mixed by Dan Alvarez
Strings and Choir recorded by John Vigran
Mastered by Mike Bemesderfer

All music tracks recorded at Companion Studios except for:
Orchestra and Choir recorded at Skywalker Sound, San Rafael, CA
String Quartet recorded at Studio 'D', Sausalito, CA
Orchestra on *Letting Yourself Be Loved* at Spark Studios, Emeryville, CA

1 **Letting Yourself Be Loved** LEW EPSTEIN
Matt Eakle, flute
Gary Malkin, piano
Richard Patterson, classical guitar
Gary Malkin and Dan Alvarez, keyboards
Orchestra (see last page of credits)

2 **Returning Home** TU WEIMING
(music excerpt from *Thousand Pieces of Gold,* Real Music)
Lu Feng Ding, erhu
Gary Malkin, keyboards
Pete Scaturro, programmer

3 **The Gift of Life** ALAN JONES
Robin May, oboe and English horn
Emil Miland, cello
Daniel Steinberg, celtic flute
Gary Malkin and Dan Alvarez, keyboards
U.C. Berkeley Chamber Choir (see last page of credits)
The Companion Arts Orchestra   (see last page of credits)

4 **Walk On** JYOTI
Gary Schwantes, cedar flute
Gary Malkin and Dan Alvarez, keyboards
Native American voices from recorded archives

5 **The End of Suffering** THICH NHAT HANH
Jeibing Chen, erhu
Phap Niem, singing monk
Gary Malkin and Dan Alvarez, keyboards

6 **Franciscan Blessing** MAXIMILLIAN MIZZI
Jeremy Cohen, violin
Robin May, oboe
Daniel Steinberg, celtic flute
Vreni Walti, Italian spoken prayer
The Companion Arts Orchestra (see last page of credits)
U.C. Berkeley Chamber Choir (see last page of credits)

7 **In Your Blessed Hands** ZALMAN SCHACHTER-SHALOMI
Richard Patterson, acoustic guitar
Norbert Stachtel, clarinet and flute
String Quartet: Jeremy Cohen (contractor),
Joseph Hebert, Emily Onderdonk, Carla Picchi
Gary Malkin, piano
Gary Malkin and Dan Alvarez, keyboards

8 **Unconditional Love** ELISABETH KÜBLER-ROSS
Paul McCandless, oboe
Richard Patterson, classical guitar
Gary Malkin, keyboards

9 **We Are Not Alone**   ARUN AND SUNANDA GANDHI
Paul McCandless, oboe
Jonathan Meyer, bamboo flute (bansuri)
Emil Miland, cello
Jennifer Youngdahl, voice
Gary Malkin and Dan Alvarez, keyboards
The Companion Arts Orchestra (see last page of credits)

10 **Be Here Now**   RAM DASS
vocals: Rhiannon, Joey Blake, Dave Worm,
Melanie Rath, Sunshine Garcia, Nicholas Bearde
Gary Malkin, piano
Gary Malkin and Dan Alvarez, keyboards

11 **The Welcoming**   MICHAEL STILLWATER
Hans Christian, Tibetan bells and gongs
Robin May, oboe
Emil Miland, cello
Richard Patterson, classical guitar
Christina Quinn, soloist
Jennifer Youngdahl, voice
Gary Malkin and Dan Alvarez, keyboards
The Companion Arts Orchestra (see last page of credits)
U.C. Berkeley Chamber Choir (see last page of credits)

12 **Swing Low**   LINDA TILLERY
Gary Malkin, keyboards

Orchestra & Choir

Orchestra on *Letting Yourself Be Loved*: originally from the documentary film *Raising the Ashes,* directed by Michael O'Keefe; recorded at Spark Studios, Emeryville, CA; John Vigran, engineer; Tony Mills, assistant engineer; Dan Alvarez, associate producer; Jeremy Cohen, concertmaster; Craig Schneider, production coordinator; orchestra members: Dawn Dover, Adrienne Duckworth, Joe Edelberg, Paul Hanson, Joseph Hebert, Jim Hurley, Judiyaba, Roxann Jacobsen, Jim Kerwin, Sarah Knutson, Betsy London, Robin May, Jeff Neighbor, Ysaushi Ogura, Irene Sazer, Jim Shallenberger, Nancy Bien Souza

The Companion Arts Orchestra, recorded at Skywalker Sound, San Rafael, CA; Greg Sudmeir, contractor; Bob Levy, assistant engineer; Dan Alvarez, associate producer; Leslie Ann Jones, Skywalker Manager; Nathan Rubin, concertmaster; orchestra members: Susan Bates, Paul Brancato, India Cooke, Deborah Dare, Dawn Dover, Don Ehrlich, Paul Ehrlich, Shinji Eshima, Julie Feldman, Leighton Fong, Joseph Gold, Lisa Grodin, Robin Hansen, Holly Helig, James Hurley, Roxann Jacobson, Katherine Johnk, Judiyaba, David Kadarauch, Mia Kim, Patrick Klobas, Emil Miland, Yasushi Ogura, Carla Picchi, Dan Reiter, Barbara Riccardi, Martha Rudin, James Shallenberger, Kathryn Stenberg, Margaret Titchener, Stephen Tramontozzi, Janet Witharm, Katrina Wreede

U.C. Berkeley Chamber Choir, recorded at Skywalker Sound, San Rafael, CA; Marika Kuzma, director; choir members: George-Anne Bowers, Tyler Bryant, Axel Van Chee, Andy Chung, Peggy Eagan, Michael Eisenberg, Michael Feola, Becky Gambatese, Helen Holder, Kate Howell, Frank Jiang, Robin Lee, Jamie Magno, Carson Mah, Bridget O'Keeffe, Benjamin Park, Bjorn Poonen, Petra Safarova, Lisa Spivak, Celeste Winant

ACKNOWLEDGMENTS

SPECIAL THANKS TO ALL WHO CONTRIBUTED TO THE CREATION AND
DISSEMINATION OF *Graceful Passages*, INCLUDING:

The Nathan Cummings Foundation
The John and Lisa Pritzker Philanthropic Foundation
The Lloyd Symington Foundation
The Fund for Global Awakening
The Sandler Foundation
The Fetzer Institute
William Harris
Bethany Hays
Steve Fox
Amy Volk, Rebecca Spencer, and Bob McNeice

Lynne Twist, Laurel Burch, and Ann Brebner

Suzanne Noe and Genevieve Malkin

Doris Laesser, for holding the vision all along

We wish to gratefully acknowledge all those who have assisted this
project, bringing it to its full realization.

SPECIAL THANKS TO OUR ADVISORS, ASSOCIATES, AND FRIENDS,
INCLUDING:
Marc Allen, Danny Alvarez, Shoshana Alexander, Barbara Aman,
Carol Angermeir, Bob Arnold, Shanna and Rinaldo Brutoco,
Sky Canyon, Beth Nielson Chapman, Courtney Cowart, Rick and
Roberta Cummings, Sofia Dumitru, Denzyl Feigelson, Lloyd Fickett,
Barry Fishman, Lynn Franklin, Fay Freed and Ron Lansman,

Jim Hollenbeck, Bobbie Ingram, Leslie Ann Jones, Alex Kochkin and
Tish Van Camp, Jean Ledoux, David Lieberstein, Mary Labyak,
Florence Marchek, Lee Ann Macdonald, Sylvia McSkimming and the
Coalition for Supportive Care of the Dying, Pat Murphy, Susan
Osborne, Christina Quinn, John Raatz, Trinette Reed, Jan Reynolds,
Ranny Riley, Cherie Robinson, Gaynell Rogers, Sam Rogers, Phyllis
and Harvey Sandler, Margaret Schaub, Butch Schumann, Craig
Schneider, Hannah Seelig, Wendy and Jerry Slick, Dan Spinner,
Skywalker Sound, Toby Symington, Georgeanne Trandum, Philea
Daria Urquhart, Stan and Devi Weisenberg, Jonathan Wygant, and
Betsy Zeger.

SPECIAL THANKS TO OUR MENTORS AND SPEAKERS,
INCLUDING:

Angeles Arrien, Chip August, Joan Borysenko, Ira Byock, Dominie
Capadonna, Deborah Chamberlain-Taylor, Ram Dass, Larry Dossey,
Lew and Francine Epstein, Ken Druck, Arun and Sunanda Gandhi,
Gangaji, Joan Halifax, Thich Nhat Hanh, Harville Hendrix, Jean
Houston, Barbara Marx Hubbard, Laura Huxley, Alan Jones, Naomi
Judd, Sam Keen, Pir Vilayat Khan, Jack Kornfield, Elisabeth Kubler-
Ross, Stephen and Ondrea Levine, Maxmillian Mizzi, Thomas Moore,
Wayne Muller, Christiane Northrup, Frank Ostaseski, Jyoti Park,
Rachel Naomi Remen, Rabbi Zalman Schachter-Shalomi, Kathleen
Dowling Singh, Brother David Stendl-Rast, Daniel R. Tobin,
Archbishop Desmond Tutu, Tu Weiming, and Floyd Westerman.

Graceful Passages includes this book accompanied by two CDs. The first CD blends intimately spoken words with music to support and ease our life transitions. The instrumental CD *Unspeakable Grace* is for those times when the music alone is preferred. It has been used extensively in home and clinical settings to create a compassionate environment for healing, reflection, contemplation, and creativity.

 Graceful Passages is a journey of transformation. Listeners can get the most out of these recordings by listening in an environment free of interruptions or other activities, including driving. A majority of the brain's critical faculties are stimulated through the optic nerve, so we highly recommend listening with your eyes closed through headphones to ensure a direct transmission to the heart. We also recommend listening with your friends and family in order to support an experience of communion with one another.

LISTENING TO THE MESSAGES

Because of the richness of the emotional content of the messages on the first CD, you may find that listening to one or two tracks is enough in one sitting. The words and music combine to support a powerful release of feelings such as grief, love, and gratitude. Many people have discovered that listening with others nourishes an intimacy that opens into safely and deeply communicating feelings and thoughts about living, dying, and the transitions of life.

 The voices speaking on the CD represent many faiths, demonstrating that loss is universal, touching all hearts regardless of beliefs. Whatever your tradition, may these journeys in words and music serve as exploratory visits to the edge of the shore we call death, whether literal or metaphoric. May they support you in a contemplative practice of the art of trusting, relaxing, and letting go.

LISTENING TO THE MUSIC

Unspeakable Grace, the second CD, is the music of *Graceful Passages* without spoken words. This instrumental recording may provide a sanctuary for contemplation after hearing the messages on the first CD or when the need to visit an inner place untouched by concepts or beliefs is stronger than the need for verbal inspiration. The music alone can carry the listener on an inner voyage and can provide a subtle background for healing and emotional warmth. Many individual listeners, families, caregiving volunteers, and health care professionals have told us that the instrumental CD provides an ideal introduction to the spoken-word CD, creating receptivity to the spoken messages.

 You may also wish to use *Unspeakable Grace* as a background to your own messages of the heart to those you teach, care for, minister to, and love. You may even choose to make a tape, for yourself or a loved one, of your own messages with this music as background.

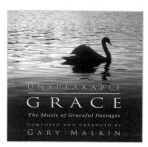

Unspeakable Grace:
The Music of Graceful Passages

For those times when music alone is preferred, we offer the stunning instrumental CD *Unspeakable Grace*, featuring the music from *Graceful Passages*, available as its own CD. *Unspeakable Grace* creates a compassionate environment for healing, and supports the experience of creating sacred space wherever you are.

Wisdom of the World produces recordings that deeply touch the human spirit. Other titles include *Winterfaith*, solo piano improvisations by Gary Malkin, and *JourneySongs*, songs of hope and inspiration by Michael Stillwater.

If you have been touched by *Graceful Passages*, please send us your comments and experiences, as well as referrals to organizations that may benefit from its use.

Contact us to learn more about our spoken-word, instrumental, or vocal music CDs, to subscribe to our e-newsletter of events and new recordings, or to speak to us about concerts, workshops, and other presentations.

WISDOM OF THE WORLD
PO Box 2528
Novato, CA 94948
Toll free: (888) 883-9060
Fax: (415) 209-9608
www.wisdomoftheworld.com

Care for the Journey: Sustaining the Heart of Health Care

Responding to the beneficial effect *Graceful Passages* has upon patients, families, and health care practitioners, the authors founded Companion Arts, a nonprofit organization utilizing the arts to provide compassionate care, inspiration, and education for people facing the emotional and spiritual challenges of transition, and for those who serve them.

Care for the Journey, the primary initiative of Companion Arts, offers programs and resources helping care professionals renew their connection to meaning and purpose, cultivate presence, and appreciate their role in helping patients face illness and death. Care for the Journey workshops, retreats, and audio resources, featuring the spoken messages of leading innovators in health care education, are widely used by hospitals, hospices, and individual care professionals. Care for the Journey audio resources deliver the wisdom of inspiring educators to health professionals across the nation, making them a perfect appreciation gift to honor practitioners during National Nursing Week or other occasions.

**Companion
Arts**

COMPANION ARTS
PO Box 2528
Novato, CA 94948
Phone: (415) 884-4483
Fax: (415) 884-4413
www.companionarts.org